HODGE PODGE OF LIFE

HODGE PODGE OF LIFE

MILDRED BEARD

J MERRILL

J Merrill Publishing, Inc.
434 Hillpine Drive
Columbus, OH 43207
www.JMerrill.pub

Library of Congress Control Number: 2023917719
ISBN-13: 978-1-954414-93-8 (Paperback)
ISBN-13: 978-1-954414-94-5 (eBook)

Book Title: Hodge Podge of Life
Author: Mildred Beard

For my Family

CONTENTS

PREFACE

My motivation for writing about some of my historical events is that I am one of the older members of our family and church. I believe it's worthwhile to record my experiences, hoping they might serve as preventive measures for others so they don't repeat some of my mistakes. Another inspiration for this undertaking came when I acquired some discarded books from the library that my daughter had purchased or salvaged. I was drawn to all three for reasons unknown to me, even though they weren't typically my preferred genre.

Reflecting on these books, I'm reminded of how we sometimes regard people in the same dismissive manner. We might overlook them, assuming they have nothing of value to contribute. Yet, as I ponder the teachings of the scriptures, they assert that each of us harbors a unique gift. Each of us is "fearfully and wonderfully made" (Psalms 139:14) and bestowed with gifts (Ephesians 4:8) as we are equipped by Him.

Shifting to a related topic, I discuss our children, from whom we might glean insights. They occasionally offer tidbits about unfamiliar matters —if only we'd listen. I believe there's merit in paying heed to our young ones. Of course, not when they're disruptive or displaying poor manners during adult conversations, but there are moments when they're keen to share. I've always resisted the urge to silence them prematurely. My philosophy has often mirrored my sentiment towards those discarded books, which I once considered discarding. Sometimes, it's wise to listen intently. Who can predict missed opportunities by dismissing others or presuming we have all the answers, rejecting others' insights? Their contributions could be valuable.

The title of this book, "Hodge Podge of Life," reflects the myriad situations I've encountered and the immense love God showed in guiding me through them. I will remain eternally grateful. We might feel unworthy, yet He continually blesses us with His kindness and compassion.

1

EARLIEST CHILDHOOD
BEGINNINGS

I was born in West Virginia. Today, I hadn't yet sent my book to the publisher. However, upon turning on my TV to C-SPAN2 between nine and nine-thirty in the morning, I was pleased to see the current governor of the great state of West Virginia discussing jobs and issues within the coal industry. This inspired me to add to my incomplete book.

I began writing my book around January 2020. The C-SPAN2 broadcast was from February 10 to 16, 2021. Now, at eighty-six, I still feel immense pride for my birth state. I was disheartened to learn of the toll of two million, one hundred seven thousand, five hundred deaths due to COVID-19.

However, his remarks about the state's recovery were uplifting.

I remember when Greyhound buses sported the logo "Serving West Virginia's Billion-Dollar Coal Fields." I'm uncertain if Trailways buses carried the same advertisement. Male members of my family, including my father, two brothers, and Uncle Howard, were coal miners. Their earnings significantly benefited our household, which brought me joy.

My early years were in Lyburn, WV. We lived there until I was about five or six. My initial playmates, Simon Peter and Carol Jean, were Caucasian. They were my sole companions since no other families lived in early-rising Lyburn. As time passed, new families moved in, but none had children around my age.

My mother and I occasionally took the locomotive to church in Earling, WV. We'd almost miss our stop, prompting my mother to dash for the train, my tiny feet barely touching the ground. Often, it would be just my mother, me, the pastor, and his wife at the church service. My brothers presumably stayed home with our father.

Our residence in Lyburn was the neighborhood's largest. Many neighbors lived in row houses in the coal camp. Our home's size was because of my aunt's employment as the housekeeper for the owner of the coal mines and their residences. This aunt was a phenomenal cook, especially renowned for her from-scratch, melt-in-your-mouth donuts. We children would eagerly anticipate these treats.

The coal magnate had hired my father, even promoting him to operate the coal-cutting machine—a position rarely held by black men. Few black families lived there initially, but as mining jobs increased, more workers arrived. My entrepreneurial mother rented out space to three such workers: Mr. Greene, Mr. Red, and Mr. Toothsweet, all of whom respected her.

In time, Mr. Greene's behavior became erratic. Once, I saw him barricade our backroom door with our refrigerator and a tub full of water, claiming he saw hostile crowds outside. His delusions often involved white individuals, possibly remnants of past traumas from the South. We lost contact with him, never learning of his fate.

Our neighborhood continued expanding, and the newcomers held my mother in high regard. I later discovered she had been a midwife for some. Though my mother's formal education ended in eighth grade, she possessed an intelligence surpassing many. She often assisted my elder brothers with their high-school homework.

Mountains flanked our home. Recognizing their potential, my mother had parts of these areas plowed. She, alongside my brothers, planted crops there. My tasks mainly involved watering the newly planted tomatoes. Come harvest season, our cellar was filled with canned produce. Alongside these, my parents would slaughter a few hogs for winter sustenance. I wasn't allowed to watch this process, which I now realize was quite brutal.

Our dog, Trixie, would grow restless, particularly when the pigs birthed piglets. These piglets, once grown, became part of our winter provisions.

As mines exhausted their reserves, people began departing Lyburn. It saddened me to leave behind friends like Simon Peter, Carol Jean, and particularly Jimmie Lou. We even had a special call to communicate across the mountain. After bidding them farewell, we moved to Ethel, WV.

BEGINNINGS AFTER MOVING TO ETHEL WEST VIRGINIA

When my family moved to Ethel, I initially had only one playmate. However, more friends came into my life over time, alleviating my loneliness. I had two brothers who spent their time with their friends, engrossed in boyish pursuits like playing marbles and throwing horseshoes. Only occasionally, when they were short of players, would they invite me to join them in horseshoes.

Our new neighbors had children, offering me more companionship. The bond strengthened when we discovered both families attended the same church: Shady Grove. Although two churches, Shady Grove and Macedonia, served our small neighborhood, we all worshipped at

Shady Grove. My older cousin and I took part in choir rehearsals. Despite our relatively young age for the junior choir, we could sing alongside the older members.

As the years went by, our neighbors had three daughters, all attending the same school as I did. Two of us even shared the same grade, making our bond even stronger.

A year later, their mother had a transformative dream. She had been suffering from congenital heart trouble and asthma. After heeding a call in her dream to visit another church and be baptized in the name of Lord Jesus, she experienced a miraculous healing. She then felt a divine calling to join the ministry. During our lunch breaks at school, her eldest daughter and I would passionately discuss scripture. Our debates, often centering on Jesus' name, involved both of us presenting our understanding based on various Bible passages. My religious journey deepened when I started attending noon prayers at Mother Perkins's home. The spiritual environment perplexed my mother, but the palpable presence of the Holy Spirit during these sessions drew her closer to God.

Moving from Lyburn to Ethel marked a new chapter in my life. It was here that I attended my first school, sometimes walking a mile or two, when our usual transportation was unavailable because of family commitments.

I never questioned why we had to walk to school while our Caucasian neighbors got picked up by a school bus. However, from the seventh grade onward, we too were transported by bus, given the longer distance to Ethel Grade School and Aracoma High.

In the ninth grade, I was nominated to compete for the title of Miss May Queen. Although I didn't win that or the Miss Aracoma title, I cherished the experiences.

After graduating from Aracoma in 1952, I was uncertain about my future. Despite preparing for college, I hesitated to enroll, fearing I might squander my father's resources without a clear academic goal. This uncertainty led me to Pittsburgh, PA, where I worked as a nurse's assistant at Riverside Hospital. The job was satisfying, but something felt amiss. Eventually, I moved to Toledo, OH, living with my cousin and her mother. During this period, I contemplated joining the United States Air Force.

My stint in the Air Force was rewarding. I maintained airmen's security clearance records (excluding secret or top-secret material). Off-duty, I cheered for the Eglin Air Force football team— one memorable experience involved traveling to Fort Benning, GA, for a match. Our victory raised fears of a potential backlash from the Army base team, but thankfully, those fears remained unfounded.

After my service, I capitalized on the GI Bill for further studies. However, when I applied, the school owner informed me of their lost approval for veterans. I promptly offered to handle the paperwork to regain the approval. Navigating the complex process allowed me to receive my veteran checks, which covered my expenses.

During my stay at the dormitory, some fellow residents attempted to sneak alcoholic drinks into my beverages, misinterpreting my refusals as prudishness. My strong convictions, however, protected me.

An unforgettable moment occurred during a three-night revival at Mother Beulah's church. Although I didn't invite my roommates, they enthusiastically attended. Their participation and the subsequent visit from a church musician deepened our bond and introduced many to the joy of gospel songs. This spiritual awakening on Court Street in Charleston, WV, solidified friendships that would later prove invaluable, especially during my first divorce. The support I received during the custody battle for my daughter was heartwarming.

As my education in cosmetology advanced, I transitioned from practicing on mannequins to actual clients. By Christmas, my newfound skills earned me $32—a substantial sum, especially given my pending school check. This income ensured a festive celebration for my daughter, Vera.

My spiritual journey continued to evolve. I attended multiple churches, deepening my understanding of God's Word and responding to the divine calling to preach. From participating in the Missionary Choir to directing Vacation Bible School, my involvement in church activities enriched my life and the lives of those around me.

3

FROM ETHEL GRADE SCHOOL TO ARACOMA HIGH

M oving from Lyburn to Ethel, I grew a little older, and this is where I began my first school. We walked one or two miles if all our transportation options were unavailable because of family members needing to work early. One of those individuals was Dorothy Turner, who acted as an older sister and mentor to me. She treated me like a younger sibling, taking me to movies in town, which was about six miles away. Dorothy also styled my hair, looked out for my well-being, suggested clothing ideas, and taught me various things typically associated with young girls. She undertook all these tasks because I had no sisters, only older brothers.

With all transportation options exhausted, as they were needed for early jobs at the hospitals, this left us walking over two miles to school. As I mentioned earlier, I never questioned why we walked to school while others in our neighborhood were picked up by a bus. As a child, I simply accepted this as a way of life.

Our current challenge pertains to our spiritual rebirth through water and spirit, which changes our perspective and shapes our renewed journey with God. Romans 6:12 instructs, "Therefore, do not let sin reign in your mortal body so that you obey its desires. Do not present your members to sin as instruments of unrighteousness, but present yourselves to God as those who have been brought from death to life, and your members to God as instruments of righteousness. For sin will have no dominion over you, since you are not under law but under grace."

4

AFTER SCHOOLING OF COSMETOLOGY

W e weren't exposed to as many racial challenges as others in our Black community, but I experienced some. I often had to restrain myself. One notable incident occurred while I was on a commercial bus returning to my service base. A man, clearly intoxicated, boarded the bus and sat next to a Black young woman. As he made unwanted advances, she repeatedly told him to stop, to no avail. Distressed, she changed her seat. When he tried the same with me, I met his advance with a strong rebuff. He soon ceased his actions, at least for the duration of that journey. This event, along with another in Flomaton, Alabama—which I've mentioned previously—were my two most challenging racial encounters during my youth.

In West Virginia, Black and white families lived side-by-side in coal camp houses and worked in the same mines. However, their children attended separate schools. At play, children from both communities interacted without racial tensions. I never experienced any racial slurs from my playmates.

Historically, during the Civil War, West Virginia and Virginia were divided on slavery, with the western part opposing the practice.

In Ft. Walton Beach, Florida, where I was stationed, there was a store in the city (the name escapes me). We airmen faced an issue: if we wanted to try on merchandise, we weren't allowed. We could only purchase items with no guarantee of fit, and no returns were accepted. As a result, we shopped elsewhere. We frequented a different store where the owner, likely from the North, allowed fittings. In places like New York, the color of one's skin mattered less than the color of one's money.

On returning from my regular job, I had the duty of distributing mail in the mailroom. Once, a man addressed me condescendingly as "Suzy." Often, Black men were dismissively referred to as "boy," regardless of age. I retorted, "No, you don't have any mail, boy." Looking back, it might not have been the kindest response, but such were our experiences then.

I recall another incident while traveling south with the United States Air Force. In Flomaton, AL, while switching trains, I unknowingly entered a "whites-only" waiting room. A tense situation ensued, but thankfully, my military uniform likely spared me from worse consequences.

Another time, while returning to my Air Force Base after my oldest brother's funeral, the train from Cincinnati went on strike. Forced to continue by bus, I arrived at a bus station with two other airmen—a woman and a man, both white. Faced with segregated waiting rooms, the pair, unfamiliar with Southern norms, attempted to join me on the "Black" side. They were shouted out by the ticket seller. They chose not to abandon me, and we waited together outside for our bus.

5

MY FIRST ENCOUNTER WITH STRANGE RELIGIOUS PEOPLE

Before the unusual encounters with those not adhering to biblical principles, I had met devoted missionaries who worked faithfully, following God's directives from His Word. They maintained their faith despite the challenges they faced. Their stories of God's intervention—how He would come to their aid—were powerful testimonies that bolstered the faith of all who heard them. Sharing experiences of God's work strengthens both the listener and the storyteller, because through testimonies, we can triumph.

These missionaries had contributed significantly to liberating God's people. They freed many from spiritual entanglement, cast out demons, and more. My interactions with seasoned preachers and missionaries, who had traveled extensively within the United States and abroad, were enlightening, especially hearing about their diverse group of Black and Caucasian missionaries.

I recall a missionary named Brother Balwe. He recounted several divine interventions in his life. One particularly notable incident occurred when he was scheduled to preach at a revival in a secluded area known as a "holler," notorious for its mysterious disappearances. There was also a saloon nearby. On his way to the church, God instructed him to warn the saloon-goers that their establishment would soon burn down. Mockingly, the bartender repeated Brother Balwe's prediction to the patrons. After the revival, as Brother Balwe and his companions were returning, they discovered the saloon had burned down as prophesied. Tragically, several people had perished, having dismissed the warning as a joke.

Throughout our conversations, Brother Balwe recounted many miraculous events from his travels. Our age and racial differences didn't matter; I was much younger, and he was Caucasian. Yet, I cherished the tales of his missionary days.

In my youth, I had several spiritual encounters. Here's one:

Early in my ministry, while seated on a friend's porch, I felt compelled to speak to a passing young woman. Although I only knew her by rumor, I felt urged to warn her against rumored affairs. She initially denied the allegations, but about a week later, tragedy struck when the rumored wronged wife shot her.

Over time, I've experienced many divine revelations and confirmations, primarily through God's preached Word. Sometimes, messages received from prophetic voices align with God's Word, but it's vital to discern their authenticity.

Relaying divine messages to loved ones can be challenging, especially when fear of their response holds us back. But such messages can be life-saving. Like Jonah's message to Nineveh, the outcome of heeding a divine warning is uncertain. Only God knows. Our duty is to obey God and not presume to know a person's heart.

While living in a New York City penthouse with a film production family near 5 West End Avenue, I received a divine mandate. As I headed to my room, a supernatural force struck me. Hearing my name called thrice, "Mildred," I understood I had to obey God's call. Earlier, the scripture where God commanded Peter to feed His flock resonated deeply with me. I knew then that I was destined for ministry. I soon resigned from my position with the family, but before departing, I was given a platform to preach by Bishop Evans. This was just the beginning of a series of spiritual confrontations and affirmations that confirmed my calling.

Navigating these spiritual waters requires discernment, especially for the young. It's crucial to ground oneself in biblical teachings and to find a church rooted in God's Word.

In my early years, an incident occurred that made me realize God prepares us in advance. In my later years in New York, I knew to avoid Bishop Evans, who approached me with peculiar treatments and attempted to introduce me to an unfamiliar art. I firmly told him that if God gave me a gift, He would also guide me in its use. Bishop Evans declared I was one of God's spiritual children. However, I found solace in returning to my faith-rooted church back home. I had always perceived Bishop Evans to be like the other devout men I had encountered in churches in my hometown and those affiliated with our church. However, their teachings sometimes deviated from God's Word. This aligns with scriptures that warn of individuals who appear godly but deny its power (2 Timothy 3:5) and those who disguise themselves as angels of light (2 Corinthians 11:12-15). The Word advises us to avoid certain individuals; if we identify them, it's best to distance ourselves immediately. Scriptures such as Leviticus 20:6, 1 Samuel 28:3, 1 Samuel 28:9, and 2 Kings 21:6 advise against indulging in divergent beliefs reminiscent of King Josiah's actions (2 Kings 22:2 and 2 Kings 23:1-15). He was a good king - Godly King Josiah, destroying all idols and idol worship. And we must follow suit in every format. Another scripture cautions that if teachings don't align with God's Word, whether due to ignorance or deliberate deviation, it's time to seek guidance elsewhere. After all, one should avoid situations where "the blind lead the blind," for they'll both fall into a ditch (Matthew 15:14).

I first encountered these unusual religious beliefs when I returned to services in Huntington, WV, in the early years of my marriage. I was a mother to one child, and my husband and I lived at 1802 8th Avenue in Huntington. One particular day, I experienced excruciating pain in my head.

Desperate for relief, I sought out an elder in the community, hoping for a prayer to ease my suffering. On reaching her home, I was met with skepticism, but when I handed over my daughter, fearing for my life, my desperation became apparent. The elder prayed fervently, and we were both overcome by the Holy Spirit speaking in tongues. This spiritual intervention eased my distress.

However, subsequent interactions with self-proclaimed spiritual guides proved less benevolent. An older acquaintance recommended I consult with a particular individual. Although she believed in his expertise, I later discerned he lacked legitimate medical or spiritual credentials. I mistakenly placed my trust in this individual, only to be met with confusing readings and rituals that bore no relevance to my experiences. He persuaded me to part with my last $15 in exchange for questionable remedies. His practices and advice were unhelpful and harmful, exacerbating my health issues. Looking back, I believe the grace of Jesus shielded me from further harm.

This man later tried to trap me again, attempting to evade the message God had entrusted me to deliver. Thankfully, the discerning spirit of a friend prevented further deception. Rumors circulated that this bishop dabbled in dark arts, further solidifying my convictions.

Lastly, a personal health scare served as a profound spiritual revelation. On the day preceding my stroke, I sensed an anomaly, a subtle hint that my time on this earth might be limited. I even detailed my funeral wishes to Elder Wilbert Butler Jr. Subsequently, I suffered an ischemic stroke and underwent prolonged hospitalizations. Yet, after relocating, the familiar surroundings I encountered echoed a previous dream. It was a divine affirmation that God always prepares and guides us, revealing snippets of our future when we're attentive to His Word.

6

NO MORE APPLES IN THE SACK

Previously, my husband and I had encountered problems in our marriage. Feeling torn, I returned to my church. However, doubts plagued me, and I needed to see an old flame to decide whether to divorce or stay in my marriage. After our meeting, I felt certain about remaining committed to my husband.

I continued my stay in Toledo, Ohio. Even before his transfer from Florida to a base in Michigan, we had considered moving to Toledo to be closer to each other. By this time, I was pregnant with our second child. Unfortunately, I miscarried in Toledo.

While in Toledo, there were rumors about a church where the prophet allegedly provided members with winning lottery numbers. The services often began late in the night. Sometimes, they played episodes of "Dragnet." Upon my return home, chaos awaited. My husband had become involved with the daughter of a man known for selling voodoo-related items in Huntington. A friend married a woman associated with the number-giving prophet, only to become a widower and remarry later.

Years ago, my mother shared a peculiar story. A man who owned an apple orchard passed away. After his death, no one could take apples from this orchard. If someone tried, an invisible force would snatch the sack, demanding they empty it. If even a single apple remained, a voice would claim, "One more apple." My mother insisted this wasn't a fable, hinting at the supernatural atmosphere of the old slave state where she had lived.

Recalling this tale, I'm reminded of the Bible's teachings, especially Colossians 3:8. It emphasizes shedding negative traits and embracing one's renewed self. Similarly, Matthew 12:43-45 warns about the return of evil spirits to an "unoccupied" soul, signifying the importance of spiritual vigilance.

It's crucial to be filled with God's spirit to prevent these evil entities from reclaiming us. As Tina once told our congregation during a consecration, "Are you thirsty yet? Full and running over." This serves as a reminder of our spiritual hunger and need to be continuously filled.

2 Timothy 2:21 underscores the importance of self-purification to become instruments of good, while Romans 6:12 cautions against letting sin dominate our mortal lives.

7

THE PENALTY OF ADULTERY

God's Word in Exodus 20:14 commands, "You shall not commit adultery," a proclamation reiterated in Deuteronomy 5:18. This commandment has both natural and spiritual implications. The spiritual aspect is discussed in Judges 2:16-17: "Then the Lord raised up judges, who saved them out of the hands of their raiders. Yet they would not listen to their judges but prostituted themselves to other gods, bowing down to them. They turned quickly from the way their ancestors had walked, from obeying the Lord's commands; they did not follow suit." Similarly, 1 Chronicles 5:25 notes, "They were unfaithful to the God of their ancestors and prostituted themselves to the gods of the peoples of the land, whom God had destroyed before them." Psalms 106:39 adds, "They defiled themselves by what they did; by their deeds they prostituted themselves."

Adultery is defined as unfaithfulness to one's spouse.

Let's delve into the biblical histories of adultery. Foremost is the notorious liaison between King David and Bathsheba, which led to:

- The murder of Bathsheba's husband, Uriah

- The death of David's child

- The incident between Amnon and Tamar

- Absalom's murder of Amnon

- Absalom's rebellion

- Absalom's defeat and death

Adultery wrongs one's partner. Those guilty of it breach their commitment. In biblical history, adulterers often faced severe penalties. David, the king who penned around sixty-three Psalms, is lauded as a man after God's own heart because of his profound spiritual longing. Despite his shortcomings, David's heart yearned for God, establishing him as a true seeker of the Divine.

Nevertheless, sins demand reparation. Those who sin might assume they've evaded repercussions, but they're mistaken. Everyone must face the consequences, whether immediate or deferred. The old adage says, "What goes over the devil's back lands beneath his belly." As the minor prophet Hosea observes, "Whoredom, wine, and new wine take away the understanding" (Hosea 4:11). He was instructed to marry a prostitute as a symbolic gesture to Israel, emphasizing their infidelity to God (Hosea 1:2).

Reflecting on my youth, I recall an incident of adultery leading to tragedy. I once warned a woman against an affair with another's husband. She brushed off my advice, only to be murdered a week later. Her untimely death left her two young sons motherless. I was still spiritually and physically young then.

Years later, distance strained my husband's and my marriage. He, stationed at Fort Benning, Georgia, as an army soldier, and I, serving in the United States Air Force in Florida, faced challenges. Our separation became a chasm, leading us both into adultery. I felt isolated from my church, from him, and any support while in the USAF. Our sins bore grave consequences, as scripture warns: the wages of sin is death, not only literal but metaphorical, destroying relationships and marriages.

Remember the old marital and spiritual happiness adage: "Don't straddle the fence." Time is fleeting, so we shouldn't be complacent. The poem "'Twas the Night Before Jesus Came" is a powerful reminder. Heeding Romans 10:9 NIV, "If you declare with your mouth, 'Jesus is Lord,' and believe in your heart that God raised him from the dead, you will be saved," is essential.

'Twas the Night Before Jesus Came

'Twas the night before Jesus came and all through
the house
Not a creature was praying, not one in the house.
Their Bibles were lain on the shelf without care
In hopes that Jesus would not come there.

The children were dressing to crawl into bed,
Not once ever kneeling or bowing a head.
And Mom in her rocker with baby on her lap
Was watching the Late Show while I took a nap.

When out of the East there arose such a clatter,
I sprang to my feet to see what was The matter.
Away to the window I flew like a flash
Tore open the shutters and threw up the sash!

When what to my wondering eyes should appear
But angels proclaiming that Jesus was here.
With a light like the sun sending forth a bright ray
I knew in a moment this must be The Day!

The light of His face made me cover my head
It was Jesus! Returning just like He had said.
And though I possessed worldly wisdom and
wealth
I cried when I saw Him in spite of myself.

In the Book of Life which He held in His Hand
Was written the name of every saved man.
He spoke not a word as He searched for my name;
When He said "It's not here" My head hung in
shame!

The people whose names had been written
with love
He gathered to take to His Father above.
With those who were ready He rose without a
sound
While all the rest were left standing around.

I fell to my knees, but it was too late;
I had waited too long and this sealed my fate.

I stood and I cried as they rose out of sight;
   Oh, if only I had been ready tonight.

In the words of this poem the meaning is clear;
   The coming of Jesus is drawing near.
There's only one life and when comes the last call
   We'll find that the Bible was true after ALL!

Source unknown (Variously attributed to Randy Story, Stormy Gale, Lou Pinter, and Audrey Patricia Woolverton)

8

JULY 5TH, 2020

Following my previous writings from July 5, I must acknowledge those I've conversed with over the years. Among them is my late cousin, Cora Snow, who has since passed on. Her daughter, Kimberly Raines, frequently shares insightful scriptures on her Facebook page. I have two first cousins: Mrs. Edna Pierson Dowe and her husband, Wayne Dowe—both in ministry—and Edna's brother, Samuel Pierson, another minister. I fondly recall their parents, Uncle Herman Pierson and Aunt Margaret Pierson.

I also cherish memories of Aunt Bessie Penick. Although childless, she was instrumental in our upbringing, teaching us indispensable life skills like table-setting, dusting, and bathroom cleaning.

To her, I owe my preparedness for my first job. Similarly, I'm grateful for Aunt Lottie Abbott. On my mother's side was Aunt Montery Drew, Aunt Alberta Lawson, her daughter Josephine (whom we considered more a sister than a cousin), and Aunt Montery's daughter, Mattie Drew. Uncles Lewis and Howard Drew were notable figures; I followed them on many childhood adventures. Their teachings, be it about cleaning, dressing, or financial wisdom, significantly shaped my life. I regret not heeding all their advice, particularly Aunt Bessie's money-saving tips. Her prudent savings—once revealed—astounded us. Despite her modest career selling cosmetics, she amassed over sixty-thousand dollars in one bank account, not counting her other assets.

My mother's influence was similarly profound. She was a skilled seamstress and canner and maintained a steady devotion to Bible study and prayer. She believed God called her to teach—a sentiment echoed in Proverbs 18:16, which says our gifts will make room for us. Her spiritual gift did just that, as she taught Sunday school in Logan and Huntington, WV. A humorous memory of her involves her spirited morning praises. At the same time, I lay in bed, her exuberant worship filled our home. Now, understanding her joy, I share her sentiment: "When I think about Jesus and what He's done for me, I could dance all night."

Our family has many spiritual leaders—deacons and ministers—ensuring we're never far from God's teachings. Over ten family members, by my count, have served as deacons in various churches, exemplifying the qualities described in 1 Timothy 3:8-13.

Our family's spiritual tapestry includes Catholic, Baptist, and Methodist denominations. I discovered a booklet highlighting this diversity, learning I could purchase a hundred copies for just eighteen dollars. My son distributed them throughout our neighborhood. For his efforts, I gave him a modest reward for acting as a young minister. During my tenure as a beautician, I learned about the Full Business Men Fellowship. Their publications detailed the diverse denominational backgrounds of individuals experiencing the Holy Spirit in their homes.

9

REMARRIAGE TO MY HUSBAND THE SECOND TIME

After marrying, for the second time, to my former husband, I learned he fathered children with another woman during our union. When a child support check he'd given her bounced, she confronted me at my beauty shop. I firmly told her, "Don't ever return here asking about funds or checks related to children you and my husband conceived." Later, because of unpaid child support, he was jailed at her welfare office's behest. To release him, I had to sign over the property from my business—a business to which he contributed nothing. Previously, I'd secured a small-business loan because of several successful operational years. With this loan, I purchased our building, furthered our working capital, and acquired more equipment, allowing for increased staffing and productivity.

Perhaps he found our city challenging, especially since a lady from the community assistance program, who belonged to my church, was assigned to his case. She never gossiped; I only learned of her involvement from a third party. This discreet, God-fearing woman must have either thought I was naïve or chosen not to involve herself.

Throughout our marriage, I never interrogated him about his whereabouts or actions. As mentioned earlier, I was preoccupied with my business, raising our children, and more. Then, one evening, he didn't come home. Through all the challenges, I'd prayed for deliverance, buoyed by prayers from church friends. Some had even suggested divorce. Yet, I confided in none. While beauticians are advised to avoid discussing politics, religion, or gossip, I refrained due to professional etiquette and my unfamiliarity with local confidantes.

Raised to take my burdens to God, I searched scriptures like Deuteronomy 24:1-2 and Matthew

5:31 for guidance. Although I'd considered divorce, he once threatened me with a knife upon hearing this. Despite the threat, I didn't believe he'd truly harm me—he'd never been violent. Eventually, he left town.

God's deliverance can be unpredictable, but His provision is consistent. I can attest that God's presence was unwavering during those solitary times of raising five children. When I later celebrated in church, a cousin remarked on my joy despite my husband's absence. I told her that true deliverance deserved gratitude, no matter its form. Having married and divorced twice, I knew our union was doomed. Years later, he proposed for a third time after his subsequent relationship ended. I declined. Although we parted ways, we remained amicable until his death.

Shortly before he passed, I experienced a dream filled with profound sadness involving my children and me. Roughly a year later, he died. Though saddened, I felt the need to speak at his service. After receiving his then-wife's permission, I shared his last words about the insignificance of worldly possessions compared to one's relationship with God. His sister and friends present felt a shift in the atmosphere following my words, crediting the Spirit of God guiding my heart.

OUR PLIGHT NOW IS THAT WE HAVE ACCEPTED THE LORD JESUS CHRIST IN OUR LIFE

O ur spiritual birth—of the water and spirit— alters our mindset and, undoubtedly, our new path. Now, it is with God. In Romans 6:12, we are told: "Therefore, do not let sin reign in your mortal body so that you obey its lusts. And do not present your members as instruments of unrighteousness to sin, but present yourselves to God as being alive from the dead, and your members as instruments of righteousness to God. For sin shall not have dominion over you, for you are not under the law but under grace."

THE 2ND MARRIAGE TO THE UNION WERE BORN 4 CHILDREN

The second marriage resulted in the birth of four more children: Yvette Cassandra, Fawnda Marie, Harold Malcolm, and Malla Jean. As Harold and I continued living in West Virginia, I opened my beauty shop, naming it Le Salon de Beauty—a French name of my choosing. I briefly served as an assistant to a Girl Scout leader while my daughter was a scout. I also took a few classes in religion at Marshall University.

In 1976, my family and I moved to Columbus, Ohio, where I continued attending the Glorious Church of God in Christ. Initially, at the intersection of Taylor and Leonard Avenues, the church moved to 886 Sunbury Road. I actively served in the ministry, singing in the missionary choir and directing Vacation Bible School for three years. Assisting me were teachers, Sis. Georgianna Eldridge, Sis. Linda Pass, and others. Many in the community also lent a helping hand. On one occasion, I traveled with one of the head nurses making her rounds in Whitman, West Virginia. We stayed in the home of Pastor Rocine Jackson, who held her first service at 1516 Tenth Avenue after being installed as the young people's leader. Mildred Atwell served as the speaker during that initial general assembly.

While living in Columbus, Ohio, I attended Aenon Bible School. Bishop Perry was the president, and I was taught by Bishop William Latta, Elder Smith, Sister Conley, and Elder Naomi Sisely—who later became the assistant pastor. These dedicated instructors provided valuable teachings.

I frequented Bishop Latta's church on Wheatland Avenue, where my son, his family, and my eldest daughter's family also attended. We participated in the all-night prayer sessions on Friday nights, which I found spiritually enriching.

Even after the Glorious Church moved to Joyce Avenue, I remained a member for over sixty years. Bishop Isaiah Hamiter served as my first pastor in Columbus, and upon his passing, Bishop George

Steele took over. Sister Linda Curtiss invited me to speak on several occasions. The church I currently attend shares the same foundational beliefs. I fellowship with the present pastor, Dr. Bernita Wright, and Deacon Richard Wright. I have known them for many years and regard them as extraordinary individuals.

I needed to direct Vacation Bible School at my church, so I organized the morning sessions to free up my afternoons. I had the support of friends and helpers. Notable individuals who joined in were Sister Clark, Sister Linda Curtiss, Sister Elizabeth Richardson, and male volunteers who worked with the older boys. The community's support was immense. Whenever we take a step of faith directed by God, He ensures every detail falls into place if we only believe.

Before my involvement in the church, I faced several challenges. On three occasions, I was accepted into nursing school but had to withdraw due to difficult circumstances. Once, my house burned down in West Virginia; another time, my car was stolen in Columbus, Ohio.

While attending the Columbus School of Nursing, I faced challenges during my final weeks of rotations. I had no transportation to Grant

Hospital, where I needed to be by 6:30 a.m. With my family unable to assist and two small children to drop off at nursery school, I was in a tight spot. Thankfully, the nursery school took my children in early, even before their regular opening hours, and they even accepted my young grandson—who was still in diapers, a service they typically didn't provide. I appreciated their support and remember they woke up early to attend church. None of the parents they helped had to bring their children along.

I worked as a pharmacy technician at Merck Medco in Columbus, Ohio, for a few years. But I felt spiritually unfulfilled.

I later moved to Raleigh, North Carolina, to be closer to my son and receive extra help caring for my daughter's three children, of whom I had custody. In Raleigh, I attended Ezra Christian Center, the same church where my son and his wife worshiped—my time in Raleigh nurtured a more profound desire to understand ministry, prompting me to enroll at Shaw University to continue my studies in religion.

I received my license from Greater Life Church. Here, I ministered alongside two other sisters in the children's church. While the primary services catered to older members, I directed Vacation Bible School at Greater Life for three years. Some Sundays saw me on the roster, ministering from the pulpit alongside other ministers. After the passing of my former pastor, Dr. Q.L. Wilson, and with his wife not present at the church I used to attend, I was unsure about my place of worship. However, I have maintained a relationship with my former pastor's wife, recalling our association dating back to my childhood when I styled her hair in Huntington.

Eventually, because of concerns about hurricanes, I returned to Columbus, Ohio, where I currently worship at Cornerstone Pentecostal Church, led by Pastor Bishop Wilbert Butler.

12

BEHAVE LIKE A CHRISTIAN

Romans 12:14: "Let love be without hypocrisy. Abhor what is evil. Cling to what is good. Be kindly-affectionate to one another with brotherly love in honor, giving preference to one another. Do not lag in diligence. Be fervent in spirit. Serve the Lord. Rejoice in hope. Be patient in tribulation. Continue steadfastly in prayer. Distribute to the needs of the saints. Be given to hospitality."

Romans 12:17: "Bless those who persecute you; bless and do not curse. Rejoice with those who rejoice, and weep with those who weep. Be of the same mind toward one another. Do not set your mind on high things but associate with the humble. Do not be wise."

Romans 12:17: "Repay no one evil for evil. Have regard for good things in the sight of all men. If it is possible, as much as depends on you, live peaceably with all men. Beloved, do not avenge yourselves, but give place to wrath; for it is written, 'Vengeance is mine, I will repay,' says the Lord."

Romans 12:20: "Therefore, if your enemy is hungry, feed him; if he is thirsty, give him a drink; for you will heap coals of fire on his head. Do not be overcome by evil, but overcome evil with good."

Romans 6:15–23: "What then? Shall we sin because we are not under law but under grace? Certainly not! Do you not know that to whom you present yourselves slaves to obey, you are that one's slave whom you obey, whether of sin leading to death or of obedience leading to righteousness? But God be thanked that though you were slaves of sin, yet you obeyed from the heart that form of doctrine to which you were delivered. And having been set free from sin, you became slaves of righteousness. I speak in human terms because of the weakness of the flesh. For just as you presented your members as slaves of uncleanness and of lawlessness leading to more lawlessness, so now present your members as slaves of righteousness for holiness. For when you were slaves of sin, you were free regarding righteousness. What fruit did you have then in the things of which you are now ashamed? For the end of those things is death. But now, having been set free from sin, and having become slaves of God, you have your fruit to holiness, and the end, everlasting life. For the wages of sin is death, but the gift of God is eternal life in Christ Jesus our Lord."

Now we must grow, not remain stagnant.

Ephesians 4:20–24: "But you have not so learned Christ, if indeed you have heard Him and have been taught by Him, as the truth is in Jesus: that you put off, concerning your former conduct, the old man which grows corrupt according to the deceitful lusts, and be renewed in the spirit of your mind, and that you put on the new man which was created according to God, in true righteousness and holiness."

Our only source is God's Word.

1 Peter 2:2: "Therefore, laying aside all malice, all deceit, hypocrisy, envy, and all evil speaking, as newborn babes desire the pure milk of the word, that you may grow thereby, if indeed you have tasted that the Lord is gracious."

According to 1 Corinthians 13:11: "When I was a child, I spoke as a child, I understood as a child, I thought as a child; but when I became a man, I put away childish things. For now we see in a mirror, dimly, but then face to face. Now I know in part, but then I shall know just as I also am known. And now abide faith, hope, love, these three; but the greatest of these is love. We do not stay a child forever in our spiritual growth, nor do we in our natural growth. In our natural growth, as we know, there are approximately five stages (some say four or five) according to Bruce Tubman."

13

1 TIMOTHY 4: 13

According to 1 Timothy 4:13, "Let no one despise your youth, but be an example to the believer in Word, in conduct, in love, in spirit, in faith, in purity. Until I come, give attention to reading, to exhortation, to doctrine. Do not neglect the gift that is in you, which was given to you by prophecy with the laying on of the hands of the eldership. Meditate on these things; give yourself entirely to them, that your progress may be evident to all. Take heed to yourself and to the doctrine. Continue in them, for in doing this you will save both yourself and those who hear you."

There will be some who will hear God's Word, and we hope there will be many. Time is fleeting. We must engage in purposeful endeavors. Time, once gone, cannot be reclaimed. A question for us all: How will we account for our time if its essence were tangible? What if we spent more time playing computer games than praying, or more hours on personal grooming and fewer on instructing our children in the way they should go, or on quality time with the partner God gave us?

What holds importance to you? We must decide now and let our actions reflect it. What does God intend for us? We have but one lifetime to realize that calling. The real question is: Are you using your time judiciously?

In any capacity, after consulting with God, who should be the foremost to receive your "yes" and followed by your pastor—always be guided by the Holy Spirit. Some endeavors demand fasting and prayer before embarking, much like Jesus told His disciples. Some challenges are only surmounted through fasting and prayer. (See 1 Corinthians 12:4-11, 1 Corinthians 12:27-31, 1 Corinthians 12:1-26, and Ephesians 4:7-16.)

Revisiting my previous statement about my stroke, common residual physical conditions post-stroke include weakness, paralysis, balance or coordination issues; pain, numbness, or burning and tingling sensations; and fatigue, which might persist even after returning home.

Stroke affects the brain, which governs our behavior and emotions. Well-loved people may still feel irritable, forgetful, careless, or confused. Feelings of anger, anxiety, or depression are typical. Unawareness of a limb or incontinence can also occur.

My stroke affected the right side of my brain and the left side of my body. An acute ischemic stroke occurred when the blood supply to a part of my brain was cut off. The onset of a stroke is sudden. Strokes can afflict individuals of any age.

Measures to mitigate stroke risk include:

1. Reducing blood pressure.

2. Weight loss.

3. Increased physical activity.

4. Treating atrial fibrillation.

5. Managing diabetes.

6. Abstaining from smoking or quitting if currently a smoker.

One should avoid cholesterol-rich foods like burgers, cheese, and ice cream. Instead, consume four to five cups of fruits and vegetables daily, fish two to three times a week, whole grains, and low-fat dairy.

Foods rich in potassium and magnesium, such as bananas, tomatoes, melons, soybeans, and spinach, can help maintain healthy blood pressure —a prime risk factor for strokes. Multiple studies have shown that consuming two servings of fish per week reduces the risk of a stroke by 6%.

My stroke occurred in April 2019, and I am still on the path to recovery. I exhibited nearly all stroke symptoms profoundly. Therapies were essential to relearn speaking, eating, and using my tongue to move food to prevent choking. I was fortunate to be treated by a remarkable team of professionals at Westminster Thurber, followed by OSU Dodd Hospital. Every professional, from doctors to therapists to aides, was understanding and supportive.

I'm immensely grateful for all the help I received, especially from my family, church community, and Bishop Wilbert Butler. He offered me invaluable advice about the importance of patience in recovery.

During challenging times in my past, like when I faced surgeries, I often sought comfort through prayer and reading. As I age, I remember the phrase "faith without works is dead" (James 2:20). Belief in God's healing powers and proactive efforts, like attending therapy sessions, is crucial for recovery. Sometimes, I push through even when I might not feel up to it. And that's something to smile about—a bit of humor for the road.

14

BEFORE THE STROKE AND AFTER THE STROKE

Before and after my stroke, certain things supported me. First, I'd like to state that one will face challenges throughout life as a person of God with a calling. One might overlook or remain oblivious to Satan as the instigator in youth. Often, you might be innocent of any wrongdoing. However, being the perpetual accuser of the faithful, Satan magnifies minor, inconsequential matters, making you feel as though you've committed a grave sin. Yet, there's nothing in God's Word showing you've done wrong or neglected any duty. When young, you study God's Word, which warns of an adversary. Though you heed the message, it might not resonate deeply until you face trials. Those moments of testing jolt us to awareness. Then, as the song goes, "Learning to lean on Jesus, learning to lean on Jesus, I find more strength than I ever dreamed, learning to lean on Jesus."

15

ADDING TO FORMER WRITINGS OF RECOVERY

Anyone who reads any part of my writings knows that it is all nonfiction. I have neither lied nor exaggerated any parts of my writing. I could write about even more encounters in my life and family, but the stories in this book—the challenges God miraculously saw me through and the deceivers He guided me through under His Word—are sufficient for now. Some of these tales might leave many of you in awe, while others might understand because of similar circumstances. Thus, documenting them for our children seems prudent. I've discussed some of these experiences with my children, always striving to convey their spiritual significance. Some might still be on milk and not meat, understanding that not everyone has the same spiritual maturity. Such is the nature of our life's trials. Ephesians 6:10-17 reminds us that our adversary is not of flesh and blood but of spiritual forces of evil. It is essential, therefore, to don the whole armor of God.

I must mention an incident involving my eldest daughter, who was afflicted with Bell's palsy around 12. God miraculously healed her. We consulted a doctor for a professional opinion. He asserted that her recovery was so remarkable after post-diagnosis that she required neither medicine nor treatment. However, he scheduled our appointment for the beginning of the week. That previous week, upon waking one day, her mouth had contorted to one side, and one of her eyes was nearly shut. During the Sunday services, we sought prayers at my cousin's church in Huntington, WV. By Monday, we witnessed God's mercy in action. Another young girl at the doctor's office displayed symptoms akin to my daughter's initial condition. Yet, my daughter was discharged that very day. This other girl's condition seemed more severe—she was practically blind in one eye, reminiscent of my daughter's state pre-prayer. It was clear that God halted my daughter's condition from worsening.

To God be the glory for the miracles He has wrought.

When reflecting on my daughter's recovery, I'm reminded of Mother Elizabeth Perkins and the divine intervention in her life. She was afflicted with asthma and heart issues since birth and relied on medicinal smoke to breathe. Yet, upon receiving the Holy Ghost, she was healed and never again needed her medicine. She was a beacon of faith, someone I cherished spending time with. Mother Perkins often mentioned her role as the National Mother of the Glorious Church—a title truly befitting her dedication. Those familiar with her would likely concur. She often discussed her experience of being filled with "Hebrew tongues." I am eternally grateful for her influence.

Speaking of healing, I must thank God for my recovery from a severely torn rotator cuff. I was diagnosed in the 1980s by a veterans' doctor. Many had misdiagnosed the injury before him. The pain was excruciating, akin to a broken arm, but initial diagnoses attributed it to arthritis. The accuracy of a Japanese doctor acquainted with war-related injuries was a boon. Through extensive therapy, I gradually recovered, as was predicted.

My inspiration to document these experiences came from a former pastor, Dr. Q.L. Wilson, who was familiar with me and my kin. An evangelist, pastor, and prophet endowed with the gift of knowledge, he encouraged me to write. Romans 12:6-8 speaks of our unique talents, gifts granted by divine grace. We must exercise these gifts diligently, irrespective of whether they pertain to prophecy, ministry, teaching, or any other service. I am grateful for the guidance I received under Dr. Wilson's ministry. His teachings shielded me from deceit and potential missteps during trying times.

At my lowest, I was emaciated, weighing a mere 103 pounds. It felt as if I had overlooked essential tasks such as eating or drinking water—an odd sensation but one I experienced. While I refrain from equating my plight with that of David's, turning to God's Word provided solace, realizing that such tribulations are not uncommon. David's lament in Psalm 102:4 resonated deeply: "My heart is stricken and withered like grass, so that I forget to eat my bread." During a church service in Logan, WV, I found the strength to resist Satan's sinister suggestions. An overpowering urge to jump into the river was thwarted by divine intervention.

Understanding the plight of those who claim to be coerced into unusual actions beyond their control, I've faced similar terrors. But by God's grace, I made it to church. When the altar call was given for those seeking prayers, Satan tried to immobilize me. But the bishop, through God's wisdom, reached out with words of healing and promise. Recollections of David's anguish in Psalms, particularly when he grieved the loss of his son, felt eerily relatable. However, God's unwavering support helped me recover from the grip of despair. Challenges, including trauma, divorce, sin, and overwhelming anxiety, had drained me. It might perplex some readers, but my former spouse and I reconciled and remarried years later. I was relatively young and hadn't fully grasped the teachings of God's Word, such as Isaiah 43:18, which emphasizes forgetting past travails. Apostle Paul's wisdom in Philippians 3:12 serves as a beacon for all of us seeking peace, purpose, and validation in Christ Jesus. Our ultimate aspiration is to hear His words of affirmation, as depicted in Matthew 25:23.

Regarding my rehabilitation, I was admitted to the Westminster Thurber Rehab Center from OSU Hospital. The severity of my condition required a Hoyer lift for daily activities. However, the exceptional care I received, encompassing occupational, physical, and speech therapy, catalyzed my recovery. The progress was so noteworthy that a recommendation was extended for further treatment at Dodd Therapy Hospital. Post-rehabilitation, I was discharged, having made a significant recovery. My mindset remained predominantly joyful, a testament to God's magnificence. Although I endured the aftermath of an ischemic stroke, its full repercussions were mercifully absent because of my unwavering faith in Jesus Christ. Multiple evaluations confirmed the integrity of my cognitive faculties, including memory. The praise and acknowledgment from medical professionals, particularly a psychiatrist, was heartening. Indeed, our God is majestic and omnipotent. Without His grace, my current state at a sprightly 85 years would be unattainable. To Him, I owe all gratitude. Hallelujah. Amen.

16

6 THINGS GOD HATES

We have an adversary.

1 Peter 5:8: "Be sober, be vigilant; because your adversary the devil, as a roaring lion, walketh about, seeking whom he may devour: Whom resist stedfast in the faith, knowing that the same afflictions are accomplished in your brethren that are in the world. But the God of all grace, who hath called us unto his eternal glory by Christ Jesus, after that ye have suffered a while, make you perfect, stablish, strengthen, settle you. To him be glory and dominion for ever and ever. Amen."

2 Peter 3:9: "The Lord is not slack concerning his promise, as some men count slackness; but is longsuffering to us-ward, not willing that any

should perish, but that all should come to repentance."

The Six Things the Lord Hates (Proverbs 6:16): "These six things doth the LORD hate: yea, seven are an abomination unto him:

1. A proud look,

2. A lying tongue,

3. Hands that shed innocent blood,

4. A heart that deviseth wicked imaginations,

5. Feet that be swift in running to mischief,

6. A false witness that speaketh lies,

7. And he that soweth discord among brethren."

In the Book of Leviticus, chapter eighteen, we are given a list of what we should and should not do since we have accepted God, Jehovah Jesus Christ, as our Lord and Savior.

Leviticus 18:1-4: "And the LORD spake unto Moses, saying, 'Speak unto the children of Israel, and say unto them, I am the LORD your God. After the doings of the land of Egypt, wherein ye dwelt, shall ye not do: and after the doings of the land of Canaan, whither I bring you, shall ye not do:

neither shall ye walk in their ordinances. Ye shall do my judgments, and keep mine ordinances, to walk therein: I am the LORD your God. Ye shall therefore keep my statutes, and my judgments: which if a man do, he shall live in them: I am the LORD.'"

Leviticus 18:22-23: "Thou shalt not lie with mankind, as with womankind: it is abomination. Neither shalt thou lie with any beast to defile thyself therewith: neither shall any woman stand before a beast to lie down thereto: it is confusion."

17

RADICAL PRAISER

I may seem like a radical praiser in service for worshiping God because He has been with me through it all. Some situations I experienced were very unpleasant and frightening. But it's amazing how God sustained me. There have been times when I looked back on it and knew beyond any doubt that His grace and mercy brought me through. I am living each moment because of Him, so I thank and praise Him in double- or triple-innumerable portions. A person unfamiliar with His goodness might wonder what's wrong with me. I used to wonder too. There were times I faced a test or difficulty, and I would go to church, finding myself rejoicing in Him even more. Then I would question myself, thinking I should be concerned about the problem. But looking back, I realize I was trusting God to solve it. And He did.

To those of you with whom I've worshipped in various churches, I hope you understand my overflowing praise for the Lord God Almighty. Sometimes the Spirit of God rejuvenated me, leading me to run in the church. However, years ago, I faced a condition where I believed I'd never walk again. I was at St. Mary's Hospital, where my doctor informed me I needed back surgery. At home, I thought I was preparing for the procedure by consuming foods like liver and other items reputed to be beneficial. My assumption was they'd bolster my blood. Later, I fasted for three days and nights. After this spiritual dedication, I noticed a slight relief in pain. At the same time, grocery shopping and thought, "If God can relieve this much pain, He can take the rest away." I shared my fasting testimony with my doctor and my decision against surgery. He acknowledged my improvement and recounted his dissatisfaction with his own surgery outcomes. Not long after, he passed away. Before all these events, I had visited the hospital three times.

Once, I attended one of my church's Ohio diocese meetings in Chillicothe, OH, right after a hospital discharge. During the service, as attendees clapped in praise, I joined. As I did, a nagging voice—akin to Satan's whisper—reminded me of my recent hospitalization and back issues. Nevertheless, I continued my praise. Suddenly, the Spirit of God surged within me, and I found myself running in the Spirit. Those health problems ceased afterward. Yet, I remain careful not to overexert myself, particularly with heavy lifting, pulling, or dragging substantial weights. Nowadays, with advice on lifting techniques available on television and billboards, there's no excuse for ignorance. I urge everyone to take heed.

God's wonder has deeply touched my soul, as in many of yours. Even when we err, He intervenes. We must proclaim His goodness and mercy so others might also accept Him as the Lord and Savior of their lives. The promise is clear in His Word: He will never leave nor forsake us (Deuteronomy 31:6; Matthew 28:20; Hebrews 13:5-6).

18

THANK YOU, GOD

Thank God, I may not know what the future holds for me, but I am grateful for my past. I've led a fulfilling life, working diligently, facing tests, and enduring trials that only You could guide me through. I'll recount just a few experiences: the memorable snowstorm of January 1978 when my grandson was born, an incident still fresh in my children's and my memory; the fire I narrowly escaped; the collapsing ceiling at 1379 Loretta Avenue; and many more. No matter what challenges the future presents, I trust You will handle them. I've been growing in my trust in Your promises as declared in Your Word. For this, I thank You, Lord. I am learning to rely on You, Jesus, recognizing that I need more strength than I ever imagined. My faith assures me that I can turn to You, the true source of power, in prayer for the strength I seek. As Your Word states, "And all things, ye shall ask in prayer, believing, ye shall receive" (Matthew 21:22) and "Therefore I say unto you, What things soever ye desire, when ye pray, believe that ye receive them, and ye shall have them" (Mark 11:24). Lord, we love You and pray that our faith may grow as You see fit.

19

GALLERY

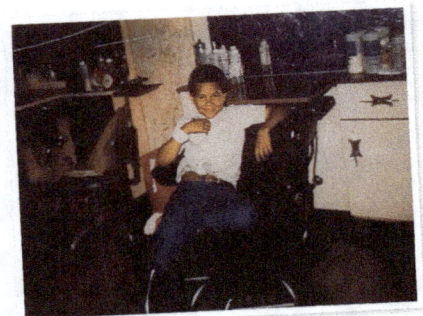

ABOUT THE AUTHOR

In Ethel, WV, while attending Shady Grove Church during my lunch hour at Ethel Carver Elementary School, I and a few classmates began discussing our differences in religious choices. At one time, we had worshipped at the same place. Still, their mother, who was a friend of mine, felt directed by God's Spirit about the infilling of the Holy Ghost and immersion in water in Jesus' name, according to Acts 2:38. After attending a church in Logan, West Virginia, and taking part in Bible class, Minister Witcher of Sharples held services in Mrs. Perkins' home. We all began attending this church, where I could feel the power of God. During a revival led by Evangelist Quander L. Wilson, I grew closer to my schoolmates and dear friends, Dorothy and Helen. We all decided we wanted the Holy Ghost and to be baptized in the Lord Jesus Christ. Mrs. Perkins soon became a minister, and I enjoyed her noon-day prayer sessions with her family. I often joined her during her visits to other homes in Holden for prayer. So much so that when I felt God's call to the ministry, her husband began calling her "Big Preacher" and me "Little Preacher."

While accompanying Mrs. Perkins in Ethel Hollow, I met a large family. Tragically, all their teenage and twenty-something daughters had succumbed to tuberculosis in the late forties and early fifties. Further down the street stood a Caucasian church. I'm unsure of its denomination, but we'd visit during the week when not in our church or Bible class.

We lived further up in the hollow when our homes lacked indoor plumbing. We'd fetch water from a communal pump for drinking, cooking, bathing, and even our Maytag washer. One day, to our shock, a lengthy black snake appeared in our kitchen window. Likely it had been feeding on my mother's eggs and chicks for a while. My eldest brother quickly dispatched it with a shotgun.

I recall another family with many young children. The father, who occasionally preached, would sometimes go on drinking binges. After his prolonged absences, his family would say he had "backslid." Yet, upon returning, he'd seem repentant and resume his preaching.

After my separation, I received my license to preach from Bishop Carl Stokes, secretary of the Glorious Church and a general board member. He later facilitated my enrollment at Juanita's School of Beauty Culture. My husband and I reconciled after working in a beauty shop near my church in Logan, WV. We moved back to Columbus, OH, where four more children were born. Balancing beauty culture, ministry, and family life, I worked in two other shops before opening my own in Huntington, WV, with the help of a small-business loan. Eventually, marital differences led to our separation, though we remained friends.

I attended the Original Church of God in Christ in Columbus, OH. I served in various roles there, including directing Vacation Bible School and singing in the missionary choir. I also traveled with Sister Hunter, our head nurse. It was a joy living in the home of Pastor Rocine Jackson, who had once asked me to speak at a Young People's Willing Workers (YPWW) assembly.

I was a proud member of the Glorious Church for over fifty years. Eventually, I felt drawn to fellowship with Greater Life in Columbus, OH. I continued my licensed ministry, directed Vacation Bible School, and worked with Sisters Brown and Edwards in the Children's Church. While in Columbus, I studied at the School of Practical Nursing. I worked as a pharmacy technician at Merck Medco, but neither brought me the same fulfillment as my ministry. I moved to North Carolina to be closer to my son and help raise my daughter's three children, two of whom were in my custody. In Raleigh, I attended the Ezra Christian Center and studied religion and philosophy at Shaw University. However, after experiencing several hurricanes I deeply feared, I returned to Ohio. Upon my return, I learned of my former husband's passing. I began attending Cornerstone Church on Joyce Avenue, where I was deeply touched by First Lady Mrs. Christine Butler's kindness to everyone, including my daughter, who had some developmental challenges. This act of love made me realize Cornerstone was where I wanted to be a member.

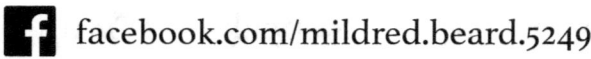 facebook.com/mildred.beard.5249